Original title:
Quieted Bars Beneath the Phoenix Dump

Author: Johan Kirsipuu
ISBN HARDBACK: 978-1-80563-415-7
ISBN PAPERBACK: 978-1-80564-936-6

The Flicker of Lost Voices

In the woods where shadows play,
Whispers dance on fragile air.
Echoes of a time gone gray,
Flickers soft, a haunting glare.

Old tales spun from threads of night,
Secrets held in tangled trees.
Voices lost, they seek the light,
Barely heard upon the breeze.

A hidden path, an ancient door,
Leading to a world unseen.
Where dreams of yesteryears implore,
And linger in the spaces between.

Hold your breath, and close your eyes,
Feel the magic in the chill.
From the past, a bittersweet prize,
Awakens with an aching thrill.

In every rustle, every sigh,
Lies the story left untold.
A flicker of the moments dry,
In the heart where love unfolds.

Veils of Dust Over Broken Dreams

Beneath the weight of time's cruel hand,
Lies a sight both stark and bright.
Veils of dust in a forgotten land,
Whisper of dreams lost to night.

Where hopes once soared on silver wings,
Now linger shadows, faint and pale.
Memories of what longing brings,
Caught in an everlasting tale.

The sun sinks low, a weary friend,
Casting ghosts over empty streets.
What was bright, now seems to blend,
With the silence of lost heartbeats.

Yet in the haze, a spark may gleam,
A flicker amidst the despair.
Reviving the fragments of a dream,
With every breath, a chance to repair.

For from the dust, new visions rise,
Shimmering with a tender grace.
In twilight's glow, a phoenix flies,
Leading the heart to a warm embrace.

Soot-Stained Secrets of Renewal

In shadows deep where whispers lie,
Old dreams entwined in a smoky sigh.
Amidst the ash, a spark still glows,
In quiet corners, hope bestows.

The heart's resilience, like phoenix, soars,
Through heavy clouds, it gently roars.
With every tear, a fresh bloom sprouts,
Soot-stained secrets, love over doubts.

The winds of change begin to weave,
New tapestries that hearts believe.
Each lesson learned, like shadows fade,
From embers warm, a path is laid.

In candlelight, a truth unfolds,
Of journeys taken, stories told.
With every breath, a chance reborn,
In soot-stained secrets, dawn is sworn.

The Lament of Lost Opportunities

In twilight's grasp, where dreams once danced,
The echoes linger of a fleeting chance.
With heavy hearts, we trace the lines,
Of paths untaken in silent signs.

Amidst the laughter, shadows creep,
In moments missed, memories keep.
The laughter fades into the night,
As hopes dissolve in fading light.

Promises whispered on softest breeze,
Haunt the corners where hearts appease.
Regret's sweet song, a gentle sigh,
Resonates deep, as dreams pass by.

In every choice a world unwound,
Each bit of silence, a haunting sound.
The heart remembers, but time moves fast,
In lament's embrace, we are cast.

Remnants of a Fiery Rebirth

From cinders black, a flame ignites,
Awakening stars in endless nights.
With every flicker, the past may fade,
But from the ashes, strength is laid.

Through scorching trials, the spirit strains,
In battle fought, true courage gains.
The fiery paths we bravely tread,
Lead to the heights where angels fed.

In shattering silence, the heart reclaims,
The whispered echoes of ancient flames.
With every heartbeat, a world reborn,
Remnants of loss, in beauty, adorned.

So rise with me, through smoke and ire,
Forge ahead, let dreams inspire.
From fiery rebirth, be not afraid,
For within the storm, new hopes are made.

Songs in the Embers

In crackling fire, tales softly sing,
Of distant realms where the heart takes wing.
Beneath the coals, a memory glows,
In songs of embers, the wisdom flows.

With every pop, a story brews,
Of love that's lost and of dreams we choose.
The night embraces with a gentle hand,
As echoes linger of a time so grand.

In whispered notes, the past entwined,
With every spark, a truth defined.
As shadows dance upon the wall,
In songs of embers, we find our call.

A melody of hope, of sorrow, of glee,
In flickering light, our souls run free.
So gather near, let the fire lead,
In songs of embers, plant the seed.

Silent Echoes of Ashen Wings

Beneath the veil of dusky skies,
Where ashen wings take silent flight,
A whisper lost in evening sighs,
Drifting through the cloak of night.

In shadows cast by flickering light,
They dance on winds of memories,
Soft echoes fading from our sight,
Like secrets whispered through the trees.

Each feather holds the past so dear,
Stories woven through the years,
With every flutter, drawing near,
Drenched in laughter, hope, and tears.

The world beneath their watchful gaze,
Awakens softly with a hum,
As dawn breaks through the smoky haze,
And all the quiet echoes come.

So linger here in twilight's grace,
Where dreams reside and shadows roam,
In silent echoes find your place,
And know the ashes lead you home.

Shadows Among the Cinders

Amidst the ruins of what was,
Shadows dance in whispers low,
Among the cinders, time does pause,
An ember's flicker, a delicate glow.

Each flickering flame has a tale,
Of laughter lost and battles won,
The memories, they will not pale,
For in their depths, the stories run.

In the ashes lies a spark divine,
A promise of new life to bloom,
Yet, shadows weave in serpentine,
Creating solace from the gloom.

With every breath, the night grows deep,
While dusk weaves dreams of silver thread,
In whispered tones, our secrets keep,
Among the cinders, where hopes tread.

So walk with me through dusty halls,
Beneath the stars that brightly blaze,
In shadows where the silence calls,
Together we shall find our ways.

Whispers of a Forgotten Flame

In corners dark where shadows creep,
A flicker pulses soft and warm,
With whispers carried into sleep,
A forgotten flame begins to form.

Its warmth, a balm for weary hearts,
A glow that beckons through the night,
As time unravels and departs,
The stars above begin to light.

Each whispered note a tale retold,
Of love that lingered, hopes so grand,
In silence cradled, sweet and bold,
Awakening dreams that understand.

The ember's dance, a gentle sway,
Invites the shadows close to see,
In twilight's grasp, come what may,
Together, lost in reverie.

So hold this flame within your soul,
For therein lies your heart's delight,
Amidst the whispers, you are whole,
A beacon shining through the night.

Hushed Melodies of the Rising Sun

As dawn emerges, soft and light,
The world awakens with a hush,
In melodies that take to flight,
Nature stirs in gentle brush.

The sun ascends with golden rays,
In whispers shared among the trees,
A tender warmth that softly plays,
In harmony with every breeze.

Awake, the flowers bloom anew,
A canvas painted bright and bold,
In colors glistening with dew,
Each note a story to be told.

The skies bloom pink, then shift to blue,
As daybreak sings its tranquil song,
In hushed embrace, the world feels true,
And every heartbeat moves along.

So celebrate the morning's grace,
In whispers of the rising sun,
Embrace the warmth, the soft embrace,
For every day's a chance begun.

Silent Echoes in the Temple of Ash

Beneath the arch of crumbled stone,
Whispers cling to air like ghosts.
Forgotten prayers on dust have grown,
In shadows where the silence boasts.

The rafters sigh with histories lost,
Each ember dim, yet fiercely bright.
They tell of dreams and dreams now tossed,
In corners veiled by fading light.

A flicker dances, sparks of grace,
On ancient walls where hope has slept.
And time, a thief, will not erase,
The echoes of the tears once wept.

Yet through this ash, a heart will rise,
With strength that comes from deep within.
For in each shadowed memory lies,
The promise of a light to win.

So tread with care on sacred ground,
Where once the flames did fiercely roar.
In silence, deeper truths are found,
In temples where we dream once more.

Embers of Yesterday's Whisper

In twilight's glow, a secret glimmers,
Soft echoes of a time long past.
With every breath, the light then shimmers,
A gentle sigh that holds us fast.

The embers whisper tales of yore,
Of laughter shared beneath the stars.
Hope dances lightly on the floor,
And paints the night with silver scars.

Though shadows creep and dreams may wane,
The fire within can never die.
Each flicker holds a trace of pain,
Yet whispers joy in every sigh.

In this embrace, we find our grace,
A tapestry of love and loss.
Each memory a cherished place,
Where light remains despite the toss.

So let them sparkle, let them shine,
These embers of our yesterday.
For in their warmth, our souls entwine,
And guide us through the darkened fray.

Beneath the Ruined Wings of Resilience

Beneath the wings once grand and wide,
The earth remembers every flight.
In every crack, a story cried,
Of soaring dreams now lost to night.

A gentle breeze, a fragile sigh,
Caresses ruins steep with time.
For every fall, a reason why,
Resilience blooms in muted rhyme.

The shadows hold a strength profound,
Where beauty thrives in crooked lines.
In every scar, a truth is found,
As nature weaves with careful signs.

With every leaf that whispers low,
The spirit stirs in soft embrace.
Each step we take, a chance to grow,
Beneath the wings of time and grace.

So let the ruins share their tale,
For through the cracks, new life will swell.
In every breeze, in every gale,
Our wings will rise, our hearts compel.

Shadows of Solitude in Tattered Streets

In tattered streets where echoes roam,
The silence speaks in muted tones.
Each cobbled stone a heart, a home,
Where dreams once danced, now lie like bones.

Beneath the lamps that flicker weak,
The shadows weave their secret song.
Each alley whispers what we seek,
While time slips past, however wrong.

Yet solitude, a friend at last,
Will cradle all the hopes we hide.
In darkness, futures unsurpassed,
Awake to dreams with arms spread wide.

The night adorns with stars so bright,
A tapestry of longing hearts.
In solitude, we find our light,
A canvas where our courage starts.

So walk the tattered streets with grace,
Embrace the shadows, let them teach.
For every lonely, silent place,
Can hold the dreams that are in reach.

Muffled Dreams in a Sea of Silence

In shadows cast by whispering night,
The stars above, they gleam so bright.
Yet dreams are hushed in misty beams,
As silence sways in muted schemes.

Across the lake, the fog drifts low,
Embracing hearts where whispers grow.
With every breath, the stillness sighs,
While distant echoes softly rise.

In corners dark where secrets hide,
The moon shall guard, a faithful guide.
Muffled thoughts in twilight blend,
Where the sea of silence has no end.

A phantom touch, a fleeting glow,
Untold tales in currents flow.
With every heartbeat, time will weave,
A tapestry of what we believe.

So listen close, dear heart, and feel,
The dreams that linger, almost real.
In tranquil depths, our hopes remain,
Like vessels lost in gentle rain.

The Pulse of Echoes Underneath the Ruins

Beneath the stones, a heartbeat thrums,
A rhythm old as time becomes.
The echoes dance in twilight's grip,
Where ancient whispers never slip.

In fractured walls, a story dwells,
Of laughter lost and silent bells.
The haunting notes of bygone days,
Intrude upon the twilight haze.

Each footstep stirs the dust anew,
Awakening dreams that once they knew.
The pulse of ages keenly throb,
As shadows play in gentle sob.

Yet hope remains within the dark,
A spark ignites, a tiny mark.
Through crumbling stone and fading light,
The echoes share their endless flight.

So linger here, in ruins' clasp,
Embrace the tales that past's hands grasp.
For in each breath, a life reclaims,
The silent whispers, the ancient names.

Ashen Hues of Twilight Serenity

When daylight fades to softest gray,
And shadows stretch to greet the day,
The world is cloaked in ashen hues,
Where twilight reigns, the heart renews.

Sky painted pale with whispers light,
Ember dreams emerge from night.
A tranquil pulse, the quiet breath,
Of day's embrace and twilight's death.

In gentle folds, the stars align,
A symphony of hearts divine.
With every glimmer, stories thrive,
In deepened sighs, we feel alive.

And as we wander, lost but found,
In twilight's grace, we'll circle round.
For in the stillness, truth will show,
The ashen hues of what we know.

So let your spirit rise and soar,
Embrace the dusk, seek evermore.
In twilight's fold, our fears will cease,
And find within the heart's release.

Silent Echoes of Eternal Return

In the stillness where time stands still,
Echoes whisper, a soft thrill.
The past entwined with what may be,
In silent moments, we're set free.

The winding paths of destiny,
Guide weary souls to what shall be.
In shadows deep, a flicker glows,
A truth that only silence knows.

With every breath, the echoes blend,
In twilight realms, they twist and bend.
A dance of fate in vital hue,
Where silence speaks of bonds so true.

The wheel of life, it turns with grace,
In quiet corners, we find our place.
Each heartbeat sings the songs we yearn,
In stillness, hear the echoes' turn.

So listen close, let shadows guide,
For in the silence, love abides.
Eternal return, a sacred rite,
In quiet echoes, find the light.

Flickers of Dawn in Desolate Corners

In shadows deep, where echoes rest,
A glimmer breaks the silent jest.
Awake, the world begins to breathe,
As night retreats, its grip reprieves.

Hope whispers soft, like morning dew,
In corners dark, it finds the few.
With colors bold, the day unfolds,
A tale of light, in hues of gold.

The wanderers rise from dreams unseen,
Their paths entwined, though lost in between.
With every step, the burdens shed,
As dawn ignites the shadows fled.

In fragile hearts, the flickers spark,
Through veils of doubt, they tread the dark.
Together hums the symphony,
Of life reborn, a melody.

The world awaits, its breath held tight,
For fate to weave a tapestry bright.
In desolate corners, joy will stay,
As flickers dance and lead the way.

Chamber of Eclipsed Dreams

In silent halls where secrets dwell,
A chamber holds all dreams to tell.
With shadows cast by light's retreat,
Hope lingers soft beneath the beat.

Each whispered wish, a silent song,
In echoes faint, where hearts belong.
With walls adorned by faded light,
The darkness stirs, preparing flight.

Through hidden doors, we shall proceed,
To glimpse the worlds where dreams are freed.
With every step, the starlight gleams,
In corners deep, we chase our dreams.

Though eclipsed by fears, the visions rise,
In fragile glow, they touch the skies.
Together forged in night's embrace,
In this chamber, we find our place.

As dawn approaches, shadows fall,
Yet through the gloom, we heed the call.
In chambered light, our hearts beam bright,
For dreams await beyond the fright.

Ironies Beneath the Dying Sun

Beneath the fading light, they dance,
With shadows intertwined, a secret trance.
Whispers of laughter, a bitter sigh,
Echoes of dreams that never did fly.

In fields where golden memories gleam,
The bittersweet taste of a shattered dream.
Hope rides the winds, but truth bends low,
Ironies linger where once love did grow.

The sun bows down, a reluctant king,
Casting long shadows where silence can sting.
Light fades to twilight, a reluctant muse,
While stories untold leave us to choose.

Yet in this fragile dusk, hearts still try,
To reach for the stars, where the lost reply.
Each fleeting moment, a treasure to save,
Ironies tell of the hearts that once brave.

As darkness descends, we ponder the past,
In the dying sun, echoes are cast.
Each waltz with fate, a radiant thrill,
To dance with the irony, we choose to fulfill.

Celestial Whispers Through Charred Halls

In halls of twilight, the embers whisper,
Tales of starlight, dreams that linger.
A heartbeat echoes where shadows bend,
Beneath the weight of what won't mend.

Celestial sighs weave through the air,
Brushing soft velvet where memories stare.
Charred walls cradle the secrets we keep,
In the silence of night, dreams softly weep.

Murmurs of magic, like phantoms, glide,
Through corridors ancient, where sorrows hide.
Each flicker of light tells of battles fought,
Yet hope remains in the lessons taught.

Through channels of darkness, the whispers grow,
Breath of the cosmos, gentle and slow.
Forged in the fires, the spirit ignites,
Reclaiming the dreams on long-lost nights.

As twilight wanes, the echoes reside,
In hearts and in souls, where we confide.
The celestial dance of all that we've known,
Through charred halls sacred, we're never alone.

The Weight of Wings Long Since Grounded

Beneath the clouds, once bold and free,
Wings of sorrow now long to be.
The weight of wishes, heavy and worn,
In every flutter, dreams seem torn.

Where skies once sparkled in vibrant hues,
Shadows gather with ancient dues.
A fluttered whisper, a broken bond,
Hearts soar alone, yet hope still responds.

Grounded by fear, their stories meld,
In silent moments, heartache is held.
The dreams of flight fade dim and slow,
Yet in every pulse, they long to grow.

With every breath, the yearning stirs,
Promises whispered as the twilight blurs.
Though wings are heavy, spirits rise,
Searching for solace beneath the skies.

In the hush of night, where dreams converge,
Wings once grounded begin to surge.
For even in weight, there's freedom to find,
The weight of wings can still be unconfined.

Reflections in an Abandoned Mirror

An abandoned mirror, cracked and old,
Holds whispers of secrets, stories untold.
Each shard reflects a time long past,
Revealing sorrows that forever last.

Dust dances lightly o'er faded frames,
Echoes of laughter and forgotten names.
In stillness, the glass captures the heart,
Each shimmer of light, a work of art.

Glimmers of hope in the midst of despair,
Reflections of souls searching somewhere.
Fragments of joy, like petals, sprinkle,
In the silence where memories twinkle.

Yet shadows linger, painting the view,
With dreams and sorrows, both vivid and true.
An abandoned mirror still holds its grace,
Through fractured glimpses, we find our place.

As night draws close and darkness entwines,
The mirror reveals where the light still shines.
In every reflection, we search for clues,
To mend what was lost, and honor our views.

Transmutations in the Aftermath

In shadows deep where echoes dwell,
The whispers speak of secrets fell.
With every change, a story penned,
In silence, dreams of broken tend.

The moonlight dances on the scars,
As night unveils the hidden stars.
With courage found in quiet grace,
Each heart will find its rightful place.

Through trials faced, the spirit grows,
Like rivers flowing, truth bestows.
In every ending, something new,
Transmuted light breaking through.

The past may cast a weighty toll,
Yet hope ignites the willing soul.
In time's embrace, we rise and mend,
A cycle endless—never end.

Through ashes cold, renewal's spark,
Illuminates the way from dark.
In every heart, a flame will glow,
Transmutations in the afterflow.

Faded Glory of a Dying Ember

Beneath the blanket of the night,
The embers whisper of their flight.
Once bright and wild, they softly fade,
In quiet strength, a promise laid.

Each spark a tale of battles fought,
Glorious moments, dearly sought.
Yet time will steal, and shadows grow,
Faded remnants in the glow.

The silence sings of what we lose,
A symphony of solemn blues.
In every sigh, an echo stays,
A memory wrapped in time's maze.

But deep within the heart's warm core,
The ember breathes, it breathes once more.
Through twilight's veil, a flicker found,
A new beginning from the ground.

Though fading now, the strength remains,
In every loss, a hope regains.
A cycle turns as night gives way,
To dawn's embrace, a brand-new day.

Tales of Resilience in the Grit

In muddy fields where dreams took hold,
Resilience blooms, a story bold.
Through winter winds and storms that bite,
The heart stands strong, a beacon bright.

With every stumble, lessons learn,
In grit and grace, our spirits burn.
The paths we tread are often rough,
But steel is forged in times quite tough.

Among the thorns, the roses grow,
Defying odds, they steal the show.
Each challenge met with steadfast pride,
In trials faced, we're never denied.

So let the world throw what it may,
We rise anew, come what may.
With stories woven, souls attest,
In grit, we find our truest quest.

For every knock, we stand once more,
With open hearts, we'll brave the floor.
In tales of old, our strength we find,
Resilience lives in all mankind.

Harmony of Hope Amidst Desolation

In desolation's heavy sigh,
Where shadows stretch, and hopes may die.
A whisper stirs in silent night,
A promise held in fading light.

Across the barren, lifeless ground,
A melody of hope resounds.
Each note a thread in fabric worn,
Together woven, souls reborn.

Through cracks of sorrow, flowers rise,
Breaking through with vibrant cries.
In chaos found, a tune does play,
A symphony to guide our way.

For in the depths of darkest hour,
We find our strength, our inner power.
Each heartbeat sings a brave new tale,
In harmony, we shall prevail.

So lift your eyes to skies above,
And dance anew with hope and love.
For even in the bleakest hour,
We bloom like roses, bright and flower.

The Undying Flame of Hope in the Abyss

In darkness deep, where whispers tread,
A flicker glows, though hope seems dead.
With every breath, the shadows bite,
Yet still, we seek the faintest light.

The heart, a spark, fuels quiet fight,
Against the waves that crush with might.
With hands entwined, we brave the storm,
Bound by the warmth, we find our form.

Through deepest night, our dreams take flight,
Carried by wings that claim the right.
To face the demons, not in fright,
But with the strength of love's pure light.

The flame shall dance, in winds unkind,
Through trials faced and bridges mined.
In every tear, a story spun,
The undying flame—it won't be done.

So hush the fears that loom so wide,
Embrace the warmth, let hearts confide.
For in the abyss, we forge our fate,
The flame of hope shall never wait.

Palms Extended Towards Amnesia

With palms outstretched, to skies so gray,
We reach for dreams that drift away.
In twilight's grasp, the echoes call,
Yet here we stand, unchained by fall.

The winds of time weave tales of yore,
Of laughter lost on forgotten shore.
Yet through the haze, the whispers sigh,
Of memories that refuse to die.

In shadows cast, we seek the glow,
Of light that strains to break the flow.
With open hearts, we dare to find,
The threads of solace, gently twined.

Amidst the blur, a spark ignites,
Through murky paths, we chase our sights.
For every moment etched in pain,
A lesson learned, a wisdom gained.

So let the past, with tender grace,
Shape who we are, but not erase.
Our palms extended, hearts aglow,
In search of life, we learn to grow.

Starlight Glimmers Where Shadows Collide

In the night where shadows blend,
Starlight glimmers, a whispered mend.
Through tangled dreams, we weave our way,
In cosmic dance, our fears betray.

Each twinkling light, a tale retold,
Of journeys brave, and hearts so bold.
For in the dark, where hopes reside,
A beacon shines, our souls collide.

With every breath, celestial flight,
We chase the dawn, we claim the night.
Through midnight's veil, our spirits soar,
Together bound, forevermore.

A tapestry of love and strife,
Stitched by the hands of dream and life.
As starlight glimmers, shadows wane,
In unity, we rise again.

So let us dance, where silence sings,
In constellations, find our wings.
With every heartbeat, we decide,
Starlight glimmers, where shadows collide.

Reveries from the Melancholy Vale

In the vale where silence weeps,
The whispers linger, lost in deep.
Amongst the sighs, the shadows lean,
In reverie spun, the tale unseen.

By gentle streams, old sorrows flow,
As echoes ring from long ago.
Each droplet holds a thought to share,
A glimpse of joy wrapped in despair.

With every dawn, the mist will rise,
To paint the sky with unseen cries.
Yet through the fog, a hint of grace,
In every tear, a warm embrace.

So let the vale, with lessons taught,
Reveal the strength that grief has wrought.
For in the depths of melancholy,
We'll find the heart of our story.

In twilight's glow, we weave our dreams,
From sorrow's song, the light redeems.
With whispers soft, our spirits sail,
In reveries from the melancholy vale.

The Hushed Lament of Lost Tomorrows

In whispered dreams, the shadows play,
A tapestry of hopes gone gray.
Beneath the stars, a silent plea,
For days unwritten, yet to be.

The echoes fade, as time moves on,
Yet memories linger, quietly drawn.
With every sigh, the heart recalls,
The fragile beauty before it falls.

In twilight's grasp, the moments blend,
Each note a story, a longing friend.
A fleeting glimpse of what could be,
A dance of wishes, wild and free.

The world holds treasure, both near and far,
Light woven deep in every scar.
And as the dawn breaks, soft and bright,
We cherish echoes of lost light.

So let us weave from shadows past,
A tapestry that holds us fast.
For in the hushed lament we find,
The promise of tomorrow intertwined.

Traces of Flight on Dusty Horizons

On dusty trails where whispers dwell,
The tales of flight, they weave and swell.
In hues of gold and skies so wide,
The dreams of wanderers never hide.

With every step, the rhythm flows,
Through fields where wild the wildflower grows.
The horizon beckons, a distant call,
To seek the wonders beneath it all.

Through shadowed paths where spirits soar,
We chase the remnants of what's in store.
Each fluttered wing, a story spun,
Of journeys started, and races run.

The stars above, a guide so true,
As night unfolds its deep velvet hue.
We trace the flight of all that was,
And in that magic, find our cause.

For every ending births a new,
A chance to rise, to break on through.
With dusty horizons beneath our feet,
The circle of life is bittersweet.

Requiem for Ghostly Visions

In shadows deep, they drift and sway,
Ghostly visions, lost in gray.
With whispered thoughts, they softly call,
Awakening dreams that gently fall.

The moonlight weaves enchanting fog,
While memories dance in the silent bog.
A requiem sung for days gone by,
In every sigh, a muted cry.

Through veils of night, the echoes rise,
As secrets hide in starlit skies.
Each fleeting glance, a fleeting touch,
Ghostly visions, we miss so much.

Yet in the stillness, hear the song,
Of spirits urging us to be strong.
For even in loss, there's beauty found,
A requiem whispered in each sound.

So let us honor the paths we tread,
Remember the dreams that softly fled.
In the quiet depths where memories lie,
Ghostly visions will never die.

The Silent Pulse of Yesterday's Cradle

In the cradle of dusk, shadows creep,
Where echoes of laughter gently seep.
The silent pulse of time bestowed,
In every heartbeat, a tale unfolds.

With whispers soft, the past ignites,
As stars breathe life into ancient nights.
Each moment cradled, tender, near,
A symphony sung for those we hold dear.

The world spins slow in twilight's grasp,
As dreams and memories weave and clasp.
In quiet corners, secrets hide,
The silent pulse, our hearts abide.

Among the shadows, solace swells,
A timeless bond within us dwells.
And as the night wraps us in grace,
We find the echoes of love's embrace.

In yesterday's cradle, we find our way,
Through whispers soft of night and day.
In every pulse and every sigh,
The silent journey will never die.

Echoes of the Unheard Rebirth

In shadows deep, where whispers sigh,
The dreams of old refuse to die.
From ashes cold, a spark will rise,
To paint the dusk with hopeful skies.

The silent muse, her soft refrain,
Calls forth the lost from haunting pain.
Each heartbeat echoes, wise and true,
Awakening what once we knew.

In hidden paths, where few have trod,
The wayward souls find peace in God.
With every step, a story spun,
Of battles lost and battles won.

The golden threads of fate we weave,
With every breath, we dare believe.
Though darkness looms, we light the way,
For love will anchor night and day.

In every heart, a flame reborn,
From shattered dreams, a new day's dawn.
With faith to guide, we rise anew,
Together bound, we'll forge our due.

Beauty in the Ruins

In crumbling stone, the past holds tight,
A tapestry of lost delight.
Yet through the cracks, a blossom blooms,
A sign of life amidst the glooms.

The echoes of laughter, faint yet clear,
Whisper of joy that once was near.
In every tile of weathered ground,
A history rich waits to be found.

The ivy climbs on aged remains,
Embracing all the past's refrains.
Though time may wear, and seasons change,
The beauty lies in what's arranged.

In twilight's glow, the ruins shine,
With stories etched in every line.
Remnants of love, of dreams once shared,
In every heart, the hope declared.

So wander through this sacred space,
And find the grace in lost embrace.
For in decay, new life will rise,
A testament to our goodbyes.

Fables from the Smoldering Earth

From embered soil, the tales ascend,
Of fire's rage and how it bends.
Each flicker whispers, soft and low,
Of strength unseen and seeds we sow.

The giants fell, their shadows cast,
Yet in their wake, new paths amassed.
For every loss a lesson learned,
A cycle grand, forever turned.

Through ashes gray, the green will sprout,
A testament to hearts devout.
In every crack, a story waits,
Of courage forged and woven fates.

So gather 'round, let fire's light,
Reveal the truths hidden from sight.
For in the heart of smoldering ground,
The fables of our past abound.

The earth reminds us of our birth,
The cycles spun, the dance of Earth.
In every tale, a truth we find,
To guide us forth and free the mind.

Journeys Through the Haze

In morning mist, the world awakes,
With whispered dreams, the silence breaks.
Each step obscured, yet faith remains,
To hold us firm through joy and pains.

With every breath, the haze unfolds,
A world of wonders yet untold.
In foggy paths, we seek the light,
To guide us through the shrouds of night.

The wandering souls, a motley crew,
In search of skies so wide and blue.
For every challenge, a lesson learned,
Through trials faced and corners turned.

With hearts aglow, we dance and sway,
Through winding trails, we find our way.
In unity, we break the chains,
And soar beyond the clouds' refrains.

So let the journey lead us on,
Through veils of mist till break of dawn.
For in the haze, our spirits soar,
To realms unknown, forevermore.

The Last Dance of Evaporated Voices

In twilight's grasp, the shadows sway,
Whispers linger, then drift away.
Memories twirl in the dimming light,
Filling the void with echoes of night.

Voices rise like mist from the ground,
Carried by winds with a haunting sound.
Each note a secret, a story untold,
A dance of the past, silent and bold.

The moonlight glimmers on dew-kissed leaves,
Where time retains what the heart believes.
A melody soft, like a lover's sigh,
In the stillness of night, they long to fly.

Fading softly, the choir departs,
Leaving behind just the echoing arts.
Yet in the silence, new tunes emerge,
From the depths of stillness, they slowly surge.

So let us cherish the dance we share,
In the breath between, love lingers there.
For in each farewell, a promise resides,
That in our hearts, eternal music abides.

Murmurs of Life in Hidden Hollows

Beneath the brambles, secrets breathe,
Where sunlight dapples and shadows weave.
Life stirs gently in sheltered nooks,
In whispered tales like forgotten books.

Softly rustling, the leaves will sigh,
As creatures stumble, passing by.
With every rustle, a story call,
In hidden hollows, life does sprawl.

The brook babbles with tales of old,
Of dreams once woven, of warmth and cold.
In every ripple lies a beat,
A heart that dances, a rhythm sweet.

In twilight's embrace, whispers unfurl,
The unseen wings of the woodland's pearl.
Life hums softly in the growing dark,
Sowing the seeds of a hidden spark.

Embrace the murmurs, the life around,
In every shadow, magic is found.
From the heart of the hollow, let joy arise,
In the tapestry woven beneath the skies.

Feathers Lost in the Atmosphere

In the twilight glow, feathers drift,
Carrying dreams on a gentle shift.
Scattered whispers from far-off lands,
Touching the sky with delicate hands.

Each plume a story, each flutter a sigh,
Of journeys taken, of spirits that fly.
They dance on currents, a graceful decree,
Painting the heavens with wild jubilee.

Once held in solace, now free to roam,
In the vast expanse, they've found their home.
Through soft caresses of breezes bold,
Tales of the brave and the many who've told.

Above the trees, in the morning's gleam,
Where sunlight beckons and shadows dream,
Feathers weave tales of loss and find,
In every gust, their purpose aligned.

So let us gather these whispers anew,
In the heart of the sky, where dreams break through.
For in the lost lies the hope we see,
In feathers aloft, we are forever free.

Ghost Notes from an Earthbound Past

In the fading dusk, echoes align,
Ghostly notes from a warped design.
Each sound a relic, a timeworn tale,
Floating on currents where memories sail.

The winds carry whispers of yesteryears,
Through rusted gates and forgotten fears.
In creaky wood, a melody lives,
A yearning heart that endlessly gives.

Pavements whisper where footsteps fell,
In every crack, a story to tell.
The songs of the streetlamps flicker and fade,
Marking the paths that the past has made.

Ghost notes linger like shadows cast,
In the corners of gardens, memories amassed.
A symphony woven in whispers low,
Where the heart remembers, and time will bestow.

So listen closely, let silence speak,
For in the quiet, the echoes sneak.
In every heartbeat, in every sigh,
Are ghost notes born, that will never die.

Melodies from the Ruins

Amidst the stones, a song still plays,
Echoes of laughter from forgotten days.
Nature weaves through cracks and seams,
Singing soft tales lost in dreams.

Wind whispers secrets of days long past,
As shadows dance, their stories cast.
In the heart of the ruins, life does sing,
In the silence, hope takes wing.

Ghostly figures appear and fade,
In the twilight, their dreams are laid.
Each note a memory, each chord a sigh,
Remnants of moments that dared to fly.

The moonlight bathes the ancient stones,
Bringing forth voices from the unknown.
Melodies float on a gentle breeze,
Waltzing with leaves of the whispering trees.

Awake the echoes that softly hum,
Life intertwined where sorrows come.
In this haven of lost melodies,
The spirit rejoices, and the soul is free.

Whispers of the Forgotten Flight

On a windswept hill, the shadows play,
Tracing the path of a long-gone day.
Stars shimmer bright, a watchful eye,
Guiding the souls who dare to fly.

Lost in the stillness, secrets unfold,
Stories of adventures, both brave and bold.
High above, where dreams take flight,
Whispers of freedom on a starry night.

Clouds drift softly in a silken breeze,
Holding the wishes that bend the knees.
Feathers brush past, a gentle touch,
In the quiet, we long for so much.

Awakened spirits, in twilight's gleam,
Colors of life spun from a dream.
Carried on winds, a tale untold,
In the heart, the embers of old.

The moon's soft glow reveals hidden paths,
Where hopes and dreams weave gentle wraths.
Leaving behind their mark on the night,
In the dance of shadows, we find our light.

The Stillness of Broken Stories

In the quiet corners of a feeble heart,
Lie the remnants of tales that fell apart.
Page after page, they whisper and sigh,
In the stillness, their echoes lie.

Words once woven in vibrant hues,
Now haunt the silence, share their blues.
Brittle leaves flutter, memories ignite,
Flickers of joy in the long, dark night.

Time drips slowly, like melting wax,
Lingering secrets that life sometimes lacks.
In shadows, the essence of dreams takes shape,
In forgotten tales, our courage, escape.

The quiet of night holds stories so dear,
Whispers of laughter drift close, yet near.
Silence hums softly, a soothing balm,
Cocooning lost words in a tender calm.

In the stillness, we gather our past,
For broken stories can still hold fast.
With each wistful glance at what's no more,
We find the strength within to soar.

Flickering Visions in the Gloaming

As the day fades, colors begin to swirl,
In the gloaming, mysteries unfurl.
Dancing shadows, flickering light,
Painting stories that linger in flight.

Against the dusk, dreams gently collide,
In the twilight where hopes reside.
Moments ignite like stars in the dark,
Casting their glow, leaving a spark.

The horizon breathes with promise anew,
In every flicker, a world to pursue.
Hauntingly beautiful, the echoes call,
In the stillness, we rise, we fall.

Voices whisper, wrapped in the night,
Holding the magic of soft twilight.
Every flicker a moment of grace,
An invitation to dance in this place.

Through the silence, visions unite,
Illuminating dreams with ethereal light.
In the gloaming, we find our way,
Embracing the night, welcoming the day.

The Phoenix's Gentle Longing

In secrets passed through embered night,
A phoenix yearns to take flight.
With feathers soft, like whispers breathe,
A soft, shimmering, vibrant wreath.

Upon the dawn, where shadows blend,
Its heart, a flame, begins to mend.
Through trials faced and sorrow met,
The past, a canvas, dreams are set.

In every flicker, hope ignites,
Past ashes, spark eternal lights.
Yet still, a longing resides deep,
In silence where the shadows seep.

To rise again, a pledge reborn,
From every loss, a fight is sworn.
Though fleeting time may shift and weave,
A phoenix knows it must believe.

As twilight fades and dawn takes hold,
The yearning flame ignites the bold.
In every heart, where dreams reside,
A phoenix flies, with wings spread wide.

Reflections on Ash-Streaked Dreams

Beneath the stars, where ashes gleam,
Lie dreams once bright, now softly seem.
In shadows cast by whispered truths,
A heart recalls its forgotten youths.

The night sky weeps, a silver stream,
As dusk reveals the broken dream.
Yet on the ground, where embers rest,
A phoenix stirs, its heart unpressed.

With every tear, the past embraced,
In whirls of ash, new hopes are traced.
Reflections glint, like diamonds spun,
In twilight's grasp, new journeys run.

Though scars may linger, time will mend,
The phoenix knows that life transcends.
Among the ruins, strength anew,
A dance of fire, a vision true.

With every flicker, dreams ignite,
Embracing darkness, seeking light.
Through ash-streaked paths, the spirit gleams,
Awakening the lost, bold dreams.

In the Wake of the Phoenix's Cry

A cry resounds through cooling air,
A soul awakened, free from care.
In fiery winds, the echoes soar,
The phoenix sings, forevermore.

From cinders high, its essence streams,
A tale of hope, of light, of dreams.
Each note, a thread, stitched through the night,
Binding the darkness, weaving light.

In specters bright, its shadow glows,
Contrasting fate, where destiny flows.
From ashes grave, to heights unknown,
The phoenix rises, never alone.

In every cry, a journey starts,
Awakening the slumbering hearts.
With wings outstretched and spirits bold,
It nurtures warmth in bitter cold.

Through trials faced, the phoenix flies,
The echoes linger in the skies.
In the wake of its vibrant cry,
A chorus blooms, as dreams comply.

Unseen Pathways to Ascendancy

In twilight's veil, where secrets dwell,
Unseen pathways cast their spell.
A phoenix soars on whispers light,
For each ascent must embrace the night.

With steps of flame upon the ground,
In hidden ways, the truth is found.
Each shadow bends, a mystic dance,
A chance to rise, a daring chance.

Among the stars, where hopes take flight,
The phoenix paints the canvas bright.
In every brushstroke, stories weave,
A tapestry of those who believe.

Through veils of mist, the spirit glides,
On unseen paths where longing bides.
To rise above the worldly strife,
Embracing all that is called life.

From ashes born, it claims its crown,
In golden hues, no longer down.
With courage set on timeless quest,
The phoenix knows it's truly blessed.

The Sound of Silence Amidst the Flames

In the hush where shadows play,
The flicker of hope begins to sway.
Silent whispers of the night,
Cradle dreams in fragile light.

Amidst the blaze that roars and wails,
Echoes of calm where courage prevails.
In the heart of chaos, a still refrain,
Glimmers softly through the pain.

Carried softly on the breeze,
A melody that puts the heart at ease.
Through smoldering ashes, souls will rise,
Finding solace where silence lies.

In the ruins of a world undone,
Hope dances brightly, a rising sun.
Through the flames, the spirits roam,
In the sound of silence, they'll find home.

Echoes of Resilience Amidst the Despair

Beneath the weight of endless night,
Hope stirs gently, ready to fight.
A heartbeat throbs in shadows cast,
The echoes of strength from the past.

In the depths where darkness clings,
Resilience writes its hopeful strings.
Each tear shed fuels the flame,
With whispers of never-ending name.

Through the veil of despair, they rise,
With dreams held close, beneath the skies.
In the faces of the weary crowd,
Resilience sings, both soft and loud.

They gather stories, threads of grace,
Stitching together a vibrant place.
With every step against the tide,
They carve a path where hope can glide.

With arms extended, they embrace the storm,
In unity, their courage is born.
Echoes of strength, forever sway,
Resilience blooms in the light of day.

Twilight Songs from the Fallen Temple

In the twilight's glow, where shadows dwell,
Ancient echoes weave their spell.
From crumbling stone and wretched grace,
Whispers of the past embrace this place.

Songs of twilight, soft and sweet,
Rise from history, where hearts beat.
Melodies of hope, woven tight,
In the fabric of the velvet night.

With every note, memories dance,
Healing scars, rekindling chance.
Amongst the ruins, spirits sing,
Breathing life into the offering.

Lost in reverie, a sacred space,
Each chord a tale, a warm embrace.
In the fallen temple's gentle sway,
Twilight sings of a brighter day.

As stars awaken, the songs take flight,
Guiding souls through the gentle night.
In the heart of the temple, peace finds its way,
Twilight unfolds with the light of day.

Ashen Heartbeats in Forgotten Alleys

In the backstreets where shadows loom,
Whispers linger, threaded gloom.
Ashen heartbeats echo close,
In the alleys where silence grows.

Footsteps linger on cobblestone,
Stories etched in a hushed tone.
Amidst the dusk, memories gleam,
Illuminating forgotten dreams.

Every corner holds a tale,
Of joy and sorrow, love that failed.
Yet from the dark, a spark ignites,
Through ashen heartbeats, hope takes flight.

In the silence, a heartbeat calls,
Resonating through weathered walls.
Through forgotten paths, the brave will tread,
Finding comfort where dreams are fed.

So let the echoes fill the air,
As ashen heartbeats lay hearts bare.
In every alley, beneath the strain,
Hope rises anew through the lingering pain.

Hushed Shadows in the Twilight

In twilight's embrace, the whispers play,
Soft echoes of night, as shadows sway.
A lingering hush drapes the cool air,
Where secrets of old breathe tales to share.

Beneath the boughs where shadows cast,
The memories dance, though the night be vast.
Stars flicker faintly, a distant gleam,
Awakening dreams from a long-lost dream.

The moon weaves silver through the tall trees,
As fireflies weave in a gentle breeze.
Each glimmer a wish, a flicker of light,
Guiding the lost through the velvet night.

In silence and calm, the world feels near,
With every shadow, a story clear.
Embrace the stillness, let your heart soar,
In hushed twilight, the shadows explore.

Flickering Shadows of the Phoenix's Grief

Amidst the flames, the shadows take flight,
A phoenix weeps in the dead of night.
Each flickering spark tells a tale untold,
Of love and loss, of the brave and bold.

In the heart of the fire, memories burn,
As the ashes settle, for hope we yearn.
The echoes of laughter, now tinged with pain,
Resound in the silence like soft, falling rain.

From embers arise, bright wings of despair,
Transforming the grief into something rare.
With each everyday flame, the darkness seems bright,
For shadows of sorrow blend into light.

Yet through every tear, a lesson is learned,
In the flickering glow, our spirits yearn.
We rise from the ashes, anew we begin,
In the heart of the struggle, our souls will win.

Breaths of Hope Amidst the Ash

In the charred remains where the world once stood,
Breaths of fresh hope stir where dark waters flowed.
Amidst the ashes, new life must bloom,
A whisper of promise in this grief-stricken gloom.

With every heartbeat, the past shall fade,
As tendrils of green through the silence wade.
Each sprout a reminder of strength yet unseen,
In shadows deep grown, where light might glean.

The air carries warmth, a gentle caress,
Encouraging voices that hint at success.
For even in chaos, the dawn will break,
Breaths of hope linger, its path we remake.

The world holds its breath, awaiting the spark,
As dawn drapes the earth in a golden arc.
With courage renewed, we rise from the ash,
In the tapestry woven, the bright threads flash.

Dreams Entombed in Sacred Ground

In silent repose, where the ancient sleep,
Dreams lie entombed in the soil so deep.
With every soft whisper, their stories unfold,
Of yesterdays forged in the secrets of old.

The murmurs of spirits, a haunting refrain,
Echo through time, like shadows in rain.
They sing of the journeys in twilight's embrace,
Of hope born anew in this sacred space.

From the gentle decay, new stories arise,
With starlit reflections like whispered goodbyes.
Through roots intertwined, the past finds its way,
In dreams that are buried, where shadows play.

For each solemn stone tells a tale to the night,
Of love, of longing, of lost guiding light.
In the heart of the earth, our dreams still abound,
A tapestry woven on sacred ground.

Where Breath Meets Stillness

In twilight's gentle hold we stand,
The whispers dance across the land.
Beneath the sky's vast, velvet dome,
We find a peace that feels like home.

The echoes fade, the world's asleep,
In quietude, our secrets keep.
As shadows stretch and silence sighs,
We breathe as one beneath the skies.

The stars alight with ancient grace,
Reflecting dreams we dare embrace.
A breath that weaves through time and space,
Reminds us here, we share this place.

In stillness deep, our thoughts entwine,
A spark of magic, old and fine.
The world dissolves, all worries cease,
In moments held, we taste our peace.

So let us linger, side by side,
With hearts unmasked and souls untied.
As breath meets stillness, night holds sway,
Together in this wondrous way.

Echoes of a Dream Deferred

In corners where the shadows creep,
Lie dreams once sown, now lost in sleep.
A distant bell begins to toll,
For hopes that linger in the soul.

Their whispers call on winds of change,
As time transforms, though paths feel strange.
The tapestry we dared to weave,
Now frays beneath the weight of leave.

Yet in the night, a flicker glows,
A flame that stirs, a heart that knows.
Though dreams may dim, they do not die,
For echoes linger, drifting by.

With tender grace, we gather up,
The fragments cast within our cup.
In silence, we find strength anew,
As echoes guide us, pulling through.

And as the dawn breaks brightly near,
We face the day without a fear.
For dreams deferred can still ignite,
A path illuminated by their light.

Remnants of the Cherished and Discarded

In boxes worn and dusty seams,
Lie remnants of our shattered dreams.
The cherished bits, like jewels, gleam,
Amidst the fray, a tender theme.

Yet cast aside, the broken thread,
Of memories we hoped to shed.
A careful glance, a wistful tear,
For all that's lost, and held so dear.

Each whisper tells a story true,
Of skies once blue, now turned askew.
In shadows deep, the echoes wail,
Of moments past, a ghostly tale.

Yet in each shard, a spark remains,
Of laughter shared, of joy and pains.
For remnants weave a rich design,
Of what was lost, and what is mine.

So let the past inform our dreams,
As sunlight spills on silver streams.
For in the mix of joy and sorrow,
Lies the promise of tomorrow.

Nightfall over Abandoned Echoes

When night descends on empty streets,
The quiet hush of darkness greets.
With every step, the shadows loom,
As echoes whisper from the gloom.

Once vibrant halls with laughter bright,
Now cradle silence, veiled in night.
Yet in their depths, a story sighs,
Of dreams that linger, never dies.

The moonlight casts a silver sheen,
On echoes that have long since been.
Through empty windows, soft winds blow,
Reviving tales of long ago.

In whispered tones beneath the stars,
We find our solace in the scars.
Each shadow holds a piece of time,
A haunting melody, a rhyme.

So in the stillness, let us roam,
Through nightfall's arms, we find our home.
For in abandoned echoes strong,
We weave our night into a song.

Timelessness Sinks into the Ashes

In shadows where the memories dwell,
Fleeting moments weave their spell.
Whispers of time, lost in the haze,
Echo softly through twilight's maze.

The flames consume what once was bright,
Turning dreams to embers, fading light.
Yet in the sorrow, hope does rise,
A glimmer found beneath the skies.

From ashes, stories yearn to breathe,
In silence, they weave a golden wreath.
For every end, a new beginning,
Life's dance continues, softly spinning.

The clock may tick, yet hearts will beat,
In every loss, there's bittersweet.
Timelessness whispers, soft as night,
In every ending, a spark of light.

Rebirth in Fragments of Time

In shards of dusk, the dawn regains,
Fragments scattered, joy and pain.
Every heartbeat, a chance to choose,
In every loss, the soul can lose.

A tapestry of threaded dreams,
Woven gently by silent streams.
With each rebirth, the shadows fade,
New paths emerge from what we've made.

The cycle spins with steady grace,
Each moment offers its own embrace.
Time reveals what lies beneath,
A treasure hidden, wrapped in grief.

With every breath, we twist and turn,
The flame within begins to burn.
From ashes cold, the warmth ignites,
Rebirth is found in darkest nights.

Crystalline Silence on Eroded Ground

Upon the earth where dreams once danced,
Crystalline silence sings, entranced.
The echoes linger, soft and clear,
A whisper carried through the year.

Eroded ground, where stories lie,
Time's gentle touch, a tender sigh.
Each grain holds memories yet untold,
In quietude, the past unfolds.

A glimmer shines within the still,
As nature bends to time's own will.
Beneath the silence, secrets hum,
A symphony from which we come.

We walk the path where shadows blend,
To find the light that time can lend.
Crystalline moments, rare and bright,
Unravel gently into night.

Parables Wrought from Ash and Feather

From ashes rise the tales we weave,
In feathered whispers, hearts believe.
Each story born from trials faced,
Parables of hope, oft embraced.

The smoke of strife, a dance of fate,
Transforms the dark to something great.
With every loss, a lesson learned,
In fragile moments, wisdom earned.

A tapestry of flight and fall,
In every echo, hear the call.
Through whispered winds, the truth shall soar,
With wings of ash, we seek for more.

Each feather falls, yet rises still,
In the ashes, dreams are fulfilled.
From parables that life imparts,
We find the magic in our hearts.

Beneath the Fallen Feather's Gaze

In whispers soft where shadows creep,
A feather floats, its secrets keep.
Beneath the moon's silvery glow,
Dreams unfurl, the night winds blow.

Lost hopes linger, like gentle sighs,
Birdsong echoes, as daylight dies.
Each fluttered wing, a tale untold,
In the silk of dusk, brave hearts unfold.

Beneath the sky, so vast and wide,
Where memories dance, they cannot hide.
An endless search through twilight's haze,
For warmth and peace in feather's gaze.

The stars align, and time stands still,
In the quiet, they weave their will.
A tapestry spun from dreams and fears,
Threaded softly through our years.

From dusk to dawn, the night prevails,
In every whisper, a heart unveils.
The feather falls, yet still we chase,
The hidden truths, the past we face.

Unseen Threads of Yesterday's Lament

In the attic, shadows weave,
Forgotten tales that few believe.
Threads of gold, frayed and worn,
Whisper stories, lost, forlorn.

Each memento, a silent cry,
Echoes of those who danced and died.
In every stitch, a heartbeat wakes,
A promise kept, a vow that shakes.

Through dust and time, the voices blend,
A tapestry where memories mend.
Yet woven deep, a sorrow's weight,
Time's cruel muse, a bitter fate.

The candles flicker, shadows play,
With each new dawn, they fade away.
Yet still they call from days gone past,
Unseen threads, in echoes cast.

In every corner, ghosts reside,
Whispering truths we try to hide.
But as we listen, we learn to see,
The unseen threads that set us free.

Flickers of Light in Dim Chambers

In chambers deep, where echoes dwell,
Flickers of light weave their spell.
Each corner hides a glimmering spark,
Illuminating shadows, soft and stark.

Beneath the surface, the heart does race,
As secrets move in time and space.
With whispered hopes, the darkness sings,
A dance of joy, the light it brings.

Through heavy sighs and tempered grace,
The spirits linger, a soft embrace.
A candle's twinkle, a fleeting chance,
Casts long reflections, each fleeting glance.

In silence, dreams begin to grow,
Illuminating all we know.
The chambers echo with a song,
Of light and shadow, where we belong.

As light shall fade, the night will rise,
Yet in our hearts, the flicker lies.
In every chamber, in each breath,
Flickers of light defy the death.

Regrets Adrift on a Sea of Dust

In the attic's gloom, regrets take flight,
Adrift on dust, in the pale moonlight.
Forgotten dreams, like ships at sea,
Sailing through time, they long to be free.

Each grain a memory, split and torn,
A tale of laughter, a heart reborn.
Yet shadows linger, like whispers lost,
In the voyage of fate, we bear the cost.

With every wave, a sorrow's taste,
Navigating hope, in silence faced.
The ocean's pull, it beckons near,
Yet still, we drown in waves of fear.

As dust collects on forgotten tomes,
The heart recalls its far-off homes.
Each tear a ripple on the shore,
In the sea of dreams, we search for more.

But as we sail on this fragile raft,
We learn through time, to make our craft.
For every regret, like mist, must fade,
Adrift we float, our fears outlaid.

Celestial Chords in the Rusted Night

In twilight's hush, the stars awake,
Their whispered songs, the moon will take.
Through silver wisps, the night unfolds,
A tapestry of dreams retold.

The constellations, bold and bright,
Compose a symphony of light.
Each twinkle, like a distant call,
Reminds us of our place, so small.

In rusted skies, the echoes play,
Of stories lost, of yesterday.
On hidden winds, they drift and weave,
A melody that none believe.

Yet in our hearts, the music grows,
As time unravels, softly flows.
With every note, a spark ignites,
In celestial chords, we find our nights.

So let us dance beneath this dome,
Where starlit verses guide us home.
In the embrace of cosmic grace,
We find our dreams, our sacred space.

Visions of Light Behind the Ashen Veil

Behind the shadows, visions gleam,
A flicker of hope, a distant dream.
Through ash and smoke, a truth resides,
In every soul, a spark abides.

The veil may cloak, but cannot bind,
The radiant light our hearts must find.
Through trials dark, we search and seek,
For whispered truths, for voices weak.

With every breath, the embers rise,
Into the realm of painted skies.
Where light breaks forth, anew each day,
The ashen veil will fade away.

We gather strength from all we've lost,
Embrace the warmth, despite the cost.
Visions of light, a guiding star,
Eclipsing shadows, near and far.

In unity, our spirits soar,
Beyond the veil, we are much more.
Through light, we'll weave a brighter tale,
And shatter dark with love's prevail.

Harmonies Lost to the Winds of Change

As seasons shift and rivers bend,
The harmonies begin to end.
In silence, those sweet notes reside,
Where echoes dance, and dreams collide.

The winds of change, they whisper low,
Of things forgotten, tales of woe.
Yet in their breath, a promise lies,
Of new beginnings, fresh sunrise.

Through time's embrace, we learn to grow,
To find our rhythm, soft and slow.
In every loss, there grows the chance,
For melodies to still entrance.

We gather echoes, stitch them tight,
To craft a song that feels just right.
Though harmonies may fade away,
New notes will come to light our way.

So let us sing, through every storm,
To find the beauty, bright and warm.
For winds of change may howl and sway,
Yet they can't take our hearts' ballet.

Mysteries Hidden Beneath the Embers

Beneath the embers, secrets lie,
Of whispered tales and days gone by.
In silent glow, the shadows dance,
Inviting us to take the chance.

The mysteries of the past, they wait,
In ashes cold, they contemplate.
With tender hearts, we dare to pry,
And glimpse the truths that never die.

In every flicker, stories spin,
Of warmth once felt, of love within.
As night descends and darkness falls,
We search for light, where silence calls.

Through every spark, the echoes rise,
From hidden depths to countless skies.
In every ember, memories glow,
Reminding us of what we know.

So gather round, let spirits soar,
For mysteries hide, yet yearn for more.
In every heart, a fire burns bright,
Unlocking worlds from dark to light.

Beneath the Ashes

Beneath the ashes, secrets lie,
Hopes once bright, now flame's goodbye.
Whispers stir in the silent night,
Dreams turn to shadows, lost from sight.

The embers cool, the echoes fade,
Yet memories linger, never afraid.
In every spark, a story weaves,
A tapestry worn, yet the heart believes.

The phoenix calls from depths of pain,
With strength reborn, we rise again.
Through the drear, a glint of sun,
To forge anew, when all is done.

So fear not the past, nor the night,
For beneath the ashes, there's still light.
In every ruin, a chance to mend,
To find the healing that time shall send.

Dreams Await

In quiet hours, the stars align,
With whispered hopes and soft designs.
The world outside may seem unkind,
Yet in dreams, true strength we find.

A canvas wide, of dusk and dawn,
Where fears dissolve and doubts are gone.
Each vision bright, a call to soar,
To chase the light, forevermore.

With every breath, the magic stirs,
As courage blooms in quiet blurs.
Through tangled paths, the heart will wade,
For in the dark, our dreams await.

Hold fast to hope when shadows creep,
For promises made in silence keep.
With every step, the journey starts,
A symphony played by hopeful hearts.

The Stillness After the Fire

In stillness lies the heart's own peace,
Where flames have danced, and sorrows cease.
The world once bright, now soft and gray,
Yet in this calm, new dreams will play.

The air is thick with ash and dust,
But from this wreckage, rise we must.
Amongst the charred, new life takes root,
A quiet strength, resilient and astute.

Through shadows long and echoes deep,
The memories sing, and secrets seep.
With every breath, the past we claim,
In silence finds the whisper of name.

A world reborn from fiery flight,
In twilight's glow, we find our light.
For after fire, though transformations dire,
Comes the stillness, and heart's desire.

Where Sirens Once Sang

Where sirens once sang, the silence drapes,
On barren shores where memory escapes.
Once vibrant tunes gave life to the sea,
But time's cruel hand left ghosts, not glee.

Yet in the quiet, a melody stirs,
As whispers of waves dance softly in furs.
The echoes of laughter still linger here,
A haunting refrain, both distant and near.

Through salty air, the winds do weave,
A tapestry bold, for hearts to believe.
In shadows cast by suns long set,
Where sirens sang, our dreams beget.

So listen close when the night is still,
For deep in the dark, the waters thrill.
Though songs may fade, their beauty remains,
Where sirens once sang, eternity reigns.

Traces of Gold in the Grime

In the grime of life, where shadows reside,
There glimmers a truth, like stars that collide.
Amongst the ruins, beauty is found,
In whispers of hope that dance all around.

The tangled weeds bear blossoms fair,
With traces of gold, the heart will share.
Through paths unclear and skies of gray,
The promise of dawn will light the way.

With every stumble, a lesson learned,
In the ashes of dreams, new fires burned.
For in the dark, the spirit ignites,
To chase the dawn, with all its delights.

So seek the gold in the grime of days,
Embrace the journey, come what may.
For life's greatest gifts, though hidden they seem,
Are the traces of hope, the birth of a dream.

Ashen Dreams in the Depths of Decay

In shadows deep where whispers dwell,
The ashes drift, a muted spell.
Once vibrant hues now fade to gray,
In dreams we weave, to fade away.

Forgotten promises softly sigh,
Like timeworn echoes, they softly lie.
Amongst the ruins of what once gleamed,
We wander lost, by yearning deemed.

Each step is marked by lingering pain,
In hollowed halls where hopes were slain.
Yet in the dark, a flicker gleams,
A whisper lingering in our dreams.

Beneath the weight of mournful night,
We search for paths to find the light.
Though decay wraps its cold embrace,
We cling to courage, a warm trace.

From ashes rise, a fire anew,
With echoes soft, we start to brew.
In whispered wishes, we shall soar,
For even shadows can dream of more.

Last Light on Forgotten Foundations

Amidst the ruins of time's cruel hand,
Where hope once flourished, now only sand.
The last light dances on worn stones,
A flicker of life among the bones.

Through shattered walls, the sun will creep,
Its golden warmth in silence seep.
Each beam a promise of days to be,
In forgotten corners, setting us free.

We gather strength from faded dreams,
In twilight's glow, the heart redeems.
With every breath, we build anew,
A tapestry woven from shades of blue.

The winds of change begin to stir,
A song of life, a vibrant blur.
Through cracks and crevices, hope appears,
To paint the silence with our tears.

For every ending, a new dawn waits,
Through velvet nights, we navigate fates.
With every rise, the shadows bend,
In forgotten spaces, we shall mend.

The Soft Murmur of Shattered Lives

In quiet corners, silence speaks,
Of whispered truths and fragile peaks.
Lives intersect in webs of pain,
Each story etched, each loss a gain.

Beneath the weight of fractured trust,
In echoes deep, we find the just.
The soft murmur of hearts entwined,
Where sorrow dwells but grace is blind.

With every tear, a lesson learned,
Through fiery trials, our souls have burned.
We rise from ashes, scars displayed,
In shattered lives, beauty is made.

As night descends and shadows creep,
We carry joys where sorrows sleep.
In tender moments, love prevails,
Under the weight of whispered tales.

In gentle breaths, we forge ahead,
With every hope, the heart is fed.
The softest murmur, life's refrain,
In shattered lives, we find our gain.

Feathers of Hope on Broken Fences

On weathered posts where dreams once soared,
Feathers drift down, gently adored.
A symbol bright in twilight's hush,
Amidst the chaos, a hopeful rush.

Through broken fences, we hear the song,
Of future paths where we belong.
In whispered winds, our spirits rise,
Past shards of doubt, to starlit skies.

Each feather dances in the breeze,
A tale of courage, of hearts at ease.
With every flutter, we learn to trust,
In all the places we think we must.

The world may twist, the night may fall,
Yet feathers guide through it all.
With every shift, we stand defined,
On broken fences, hope aligned.

As dawn awakens with hues so bright,
We gather dreams in morning light.
With whispers soft and courage dense,
We'll mend the world from broken fence.